Perspectives on Cultural and Creative Industries

Dr. F.D.J. Grotenhuis
With contributions from B. Fesel

Colofon

Perspectives on Cultural and Creative Industries
© 2020 F.D.J. Grotenhuis, Amersfoort

Text - F.D.J. Grotenhuis,
Bernd Fesel (co-author of two chapters)

Design - Op de Millimeter
Photos - F.D.J. Grotenhuis, 123RF

Publisher - Lulu.com

Most of the contributions in this book have been
published previously on the websites of the European
Creative Business Network[1] and Grotenhuis Organisatie-
advies bv[2] in the period July 2016 to May 2020.

E. frits@grotenhuisadviseert.nl
l. www.grotenhuisadviseert.nl

Supported by

European Creative
Business Network

First print - August 2020
ISBN 978-1-71679-197-0

"The creative industries are not only an important economic factor in themselves, they also fuel the economy with knowledge and dynamism"

European Commission Directorate for Enterprise (2010)

Table of contents

Foreword

Dear reader,

The creative and cultural industries and Europe's creators are a key driver of reindustrialisation in Europe, manufacturing, innovative services and employment: more than 12 million Europeans work in the cultural and creative industries, accounting for 7.5% of the active population in Europe.

Hidden underestimated in wider public, but for leading innovators and businesses CCI is at forefront of innovation and cross-innovation. Particularly affected by digitization, these sectors are a driving force of economic growth and generate positive spill over effect for innovation in other industries, e.g. the wider use of design in manufacturing industries, adding values to products, services, processes, and market structures.

There are many impressive examples combining Arts and Health, IT and Design or Architecture and Smart City concepts.

Many books have been published over the years on CCIs but this book presents a comprehensive kaleidoscope of insights, ranging from international good practices, to regional examples and alternative perspectives and also addresses policy making in the EU on CCI.

While the economic and innovative potential still remains largely untapped, a lot has been achieved on EU level in the past 5 years. In the eighth legislative term, the European Parliament alongside the European Commission focused on digitalization and its impact on the cultural and creative industries, the new copyright rules, the geo-blocking regulation and the design of relevant funding programmes such as Horizon Europe, Digital Europe, Creative Europe and InvestEU.

For the first time in history research efforts in the creative sector have been strengthened by creating a cluster dedicated only to research and innovation in the field of cultural heritage and creativity. The cultural and creative sectors feature in one of the Horizon Europe programme's clusters (Article 3.1 (2) (b) "cluster 'Culture, Creativity and Inclusive Society', as described in Annex I, Pillar II, section 2").

Since very recently, the Creative and Cultural Industries feature among the 14 strategic ecosystems for Europe identified by the European Commission.

In the coming years, we should make CCIs an integral part of the conversation on new technology-driven challenges and benefit from their innovative power when developing solutions in the fields of artificial intelligence, climate change and green economy.

We need to invest in disruptive innovation in particular after the corona crisis: Let's make us of the momentum and instead rebuilding the old - let's build the new!

Dr. Christian Ehler, Member of European Parliament
Committee on Industry, Research and Energy, Committee on Culture and Education, Rapporteur European Institute for Innovation and Technology, Horizon Europe.

Good practices - regional and national

In this section, cultural and creative industries in the Netherlands are pictured from a birds' eye view and next put in context of the corona crisis. Furthermore, the role of creative industries in other economic and societal sectors is illustrated. Finally, regional good practices are described in the health sector, in new technologies and behavior, and in the fashion industry.

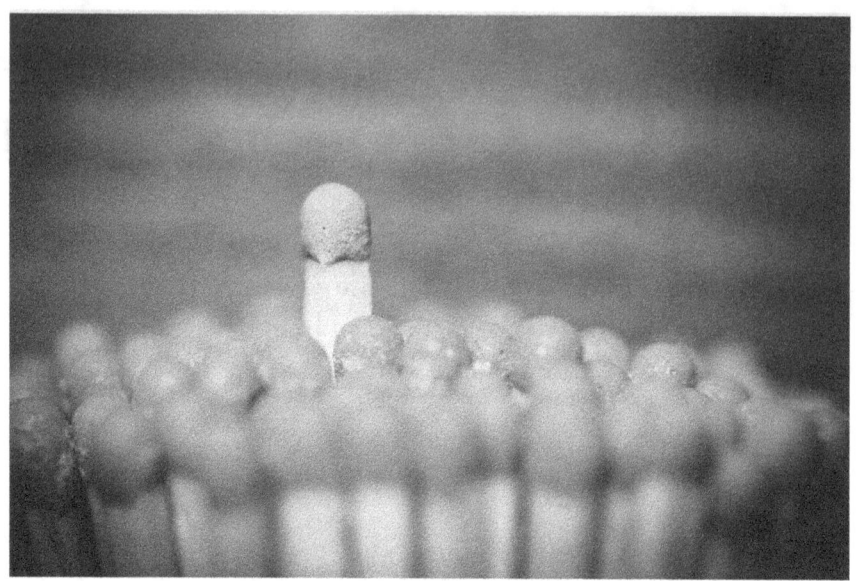

Creative industries in the Netherlands

In the Netherlands nine so-called topsectors have been appointed by the Minister of Economic Affairs in order to ensure a strong economic infrastructure, now and in the future. These topsectors consist of both old - often large-scale - sectors such as chemicals, as well as relatively new sectors. Creative Industries is one of these new dynamic topsectors that is very promising for an innovative society.

Richard Florida gained worldwide attention in 2002 with his book about the rise of the creative class. Shortly after that, the city of Amsterdam initiated the first policy actions at a regional level to stimulate creative talent. At a national level creative industries became a so-called key-area in 2004. With this label creative industries became an important topic for policy makers.

In 2005, the Ministry of Economic Affairs together with the Ministry of Education, Culture and Science developed national policy instruments stimulating creative industries specifically. At a regional level - sometimes experimental - project initiatives were supported. At a national level projects were supported that aimed at better coordination and organization of the sector. Other efforts were geared at professionalization of cultural management, solving issues concerning intellectual property and internationalization.

In the period 2003-2006, first policy instruments were developed and experimented with to support creative industries. This was an important phase. Between 2007-2011, the first national initiatives and platforms were initiated. Next, national research and innovation programs were started, further strenghtening the creative infrastructure and knowledge base in the Netherlands.

In 2011, Creative Industries became one of the nine topsectors. Over the past years, national knowledge and innovation agendas have been developed, resulting into many new public-private partnerships research projects. This way, relevant knowledge was developed and insights were gained for both creative industries and knowledge institutes, as well as for private partners organizations.

Nowadays, Creative Industries represent about 2-3% of the Dutch GNP, making it the smallest topsector. At the same time, Creative Industries is the largest topsector with regards to the amount of more than 150.000 companies. These numbers already indicate the strength and weakness of this sector: very innovative and flexible with a long tail of SMEs, but difficult to organize and to manage (sustainable) growth.

First date of publication: July 22, 2016

Dutch creative industries in times of corona

Volume creative industries
In 2020, creative industries in the Netherlands represent around 4% of the employment and approximately 11% of the creative organizations.[3] At a European scale, around 7,5% of the working population is employed in the cultural and creative sectors, equaling about 12 million people.[4] In short, creative industries represent a substantial contribution to our economy and society.

Next to a direct economic value, cultural and creative industries have a wider contribution to society: to stimulate the innovative capacity ranging from entrepreneurship (as an engine for the economy) and the design of the physical environment, to the social cohesion and branding of the Netherlands.[5]

Contribution to societal challenges

Creative industries as a sector characterizes herself by taking different angles to find solutions for challenges. End-users, instead of for instance technology, are placed central in the search for solutions. In this way, the sector contributes to societal challenges such as energy transition, the care sector, or built environment. For instance, in spatial challenges, in relation to (experiencing) the physical environment, designers and construction companies more often work together.

The Dutch Chief Government Architecture Mr. Alkemade said: *"Designers posses some essential creative skills: imagination, connection, and innovation. They are in a position to take a longer-term perspective. This is essential for the transitions that our society faces."*[6] This quotation is derived in the context of the national dialogue building culture on March 5, 2020, organized by Kunsten'92 and the Federation Spatial Quality. Similarily, the Branch association for Dutch Architects and the Chief Government Architecture provided the first annual report about the spatial design sector to the Minister of Culture on February 19, 2020.

Corona crisis

With the current corona crisis, the cultural and creative sectors face an unprecedented situation. The strength of a small-scale, flexible, and innovative sector can be a weakness in times of crisis: many independent creative entrepreneurs are in trouble. Where creative entrepreneurs were hired by large companies, they are the first being cut now. Several branches in the cultural and creative sectors, varying from the event sector to the pop industry, experience direct challenges.

According to the Dutch national newspaper NRC from April 1, 2020 a 3,5 billion euro drop in turnover is expected in the event sector. This implies that 48.000 jobs, almost half of the 100.000 jobs in this sector, are at stake. Besides performances that are cancelled, musicians hardly earn money anymore for licensed music in restaurants or hair dressors. The organization Buma/Stemra (representing the interests of music authors), together with Sena (representing the rights of performers and producers) and the government, developed a first plan and fund to make early payments possible.[7] Other branches might survive a bit longer, but the situation is very uncertain.

Tailorized measures
The challenge for the government is to take generic measures, that are also supported and partly initiated by the Dutch employers organizations VNO-NCW and MKB Nederland. On February 17, 2020 the Dutch government announced a crisis package of fiscal and financial measures to support jobs and the economy.[8] Next to these more generic measures, the Minister of Culture also took specific measures for the cultural sector, although too limited so far.

On March 30, 2020, the corona taskforce cultural and creative sectors (consisting of the Federation Creative Industries, Federation Culture, The Creative Coalition, Platform Cultural Heritage and Kunsten'92) sent a letter to the government proposing to extend specific measures as parts of the cultural and creative sector could not make use of the regulations.[9]

Solidarity

Next to these measures it is important that the economy is supported where possible and that the government remains fulfilling her role as a client for the cultural and creative sector. Solidarity, tailorized measures, and flexibility are key to preserve the fundaments of our cultural and creative sector, especially in case the crisis will last for a longer period.

From 2008-2018, Dutch creative industries, together with the ICT sector represented 25% of the growth in employment.[10] This innovative sector will be able to function as an important motor for our economy after the crisis, unless the fundament of the cultural and creative sectors has been diminished too far.

First date of publication: April 2, 2020

Cross-overs as an instrument towards a creative economy?

In the Netherlands, the Ministry of Education, Culture and Science together with the Ministry of Economic Affairs developed policy in order to stimulate creative industries. These two ministries represent the two sides of the same coin in relation to the discussion about culture and economy. On the one hand cultural entrepreneurs and artists should be able to work in an autonomous manner; on the other hand, interaction and taking customer perspectives into account help a lot in realizing business out of new creations.

The challenge is to bridge the different worlds of 'culture' and 'economy' in such a way that they strengthen each other. Collaboration in cross-overs could result in bringing culture and economy together. Creative industries already contribute 2-3% of the

Dutch GNP. At the same time, in an indirect way, creative industries have a far larger impact on the GNP via cross-overs to other economic and societal domains. The following project examples in the Netherlands illustrate the added value of creative industies to other sectors.

ENABLING ELDERLY PEOPLE AT HOME

Re-designing home situations in order to enable people with dementia to function at home as long as possible. How to design home or care environments for elderly people? What role can media and ICT (e-health) play in optimizing the home situation without being too obtrusive and taking privacy matters into account. Especially people with a degenerative disease function best in their well-known home environment where they feel happy and intuitively or automatically know their way. By moving to another care situation they can really get 'lost'. Next to the societal aim of enabling people to stay at home, there is an economic benefit in cost reduction for care environments.

DEVELOPING A 'CUSTOMER JOURNEY' AT AIRPORTS

Airports do not always allow an efficient throughput of travellers. Travellers often loose a lot of time from their arrival at the airport to their departure (entering the airplane itself). How can travellers be guided in a more adaptive, pleasant, and efficient way? Starting with the traveller in mind, a 'customer journey' can be developed. This does not only result in happy travellers, but also minimizes the costs of delays for airports as well as travellers.

TOWARDS SUSTAINABLE DRIVING BEHAVIOR

Applying gamification concepts for truck drivers in order to stimulate more sustainable driving behavior and safe fuel costs. How can gamification methods support and stimulate truck drivers to change their driving behavior? First the motivation of the drivers (users) should be investigated to be able to develop an application, based on gamification principles, that really works. Early pilot studies showed that by adding elements of competition and bonuses, behavior can be modified and fuel costs reduced on a sustainable basis.

It proofs to be challenging to find strong evidence and especially quantitative support for the precise added value of creatives to other sectors. This starts with creating awareness in other sectors about the relevance and potential that creative industries can add. Creative industries should prove their added value again and again to their customers. Experimentation with new business models is part of this journey. Governments should support the development of cross-overs as creative industries are an important driver for future innovation.

First date of publication: October 5, 2016

Thanks to
Walter Amerika, U Create

Creative industries at a regional level: U Create

Creative industries are stimulated at a European, national, and regional level. At a European level, some policy instruments are specifically geared at creative industries, think of Creative Europe. In the Netherlands, at a national level creative industries is one of the nine so-called topsectors. As such, generic policy instruments have been developed for topsector policy, though not specifically for creative industries. At a regional level in the Netherlands, policy making towards creative industries varies. Some regions, such as the metropolitan area of Amsterdam have supported creative industries as a specific sector for many years. In other regions, more generic instruments were supportive.

In Utrecht (the 4th largest city in the center of the Netherlands), creative industries have been stimulated for several years with a focus on supporting games, and media and ICT. One of the spin-offs is the Dutch Game Garden, a hotbed for game entrepreneurs.

Utrecht knows a diverse economy with many service organizations, e.g. banks, ICT companies, and care organizations.

Another recent regional initiative is the development of the center of expertise U Create.[11] This center of expertise aims at the cross-over between creative industries and health and well-being. U Create is a public-private partnership between two applied universities (HU and HKU), the University Medical Center Utrecht UMCU, and several private organizations such as Rabobank and ICT company Ordina.

U Create is also partner in the national platform Create Health, an initiative of the topsectors Creative Industries and Life Sciences and Health. This collaboration has already resulted in a first joint national research program. This program aims at enabling people with a (chronic) disease, such as dementia, to stay at home.

In the cross-over between creative industries and health and well-being, U Create moves from 'Efficiency and Effectivity' in the health and well-being sector to 'Empathy and Emotion'. This is where creative industries can add value. Next to efficient and effective operations and organizations, people often forget about the patient, who should be placed central. What are the needs of a patient? What does the patient experience? How to create a 'customer/patient journey' in a hospital environment? The need to place the patient central is being illustrated in the following project example of children with cancer.

PARTICIPATIVE DESIGN IN PEDIATRIC ONCOLOGY[12]

In order to increase the chance of surviving cancer and improve the quality of life during treatments, it is very important that patients exercise and follow a healthy diet. This is often problematic and may result in an increased fat mass and a decreased muscle mass. The central question in this project was how to stimulate children with cancer to exercise and stick to a healthy diet?

Professionals often lack knowledge or validated interventions to stimulate especially young patients. Within this project existing knowledge on health, behavior, and design is combined. Different interventions have been developed with the help of participative design methods. With techniques where children could make use of a diary, photos or pictures, all participants could communicate with each other about applicability and support for possible solutions without technical jargon or emotional barriers.

This type of project is where U Create can add value by stimulating applied research and innovation projects where creatives work together with organizations in cure, care, or prevention. U Create functions as a committed 'connector' for students and start-ups, private organizations, research organizations, and organizations in the health and well-being sector. With its funding possibilities, a strong knowledge base and a network in both worlds, U Create can make strong connections between creative industries and health and well-being. What started as a regional initiative, now has a growing national impact and even an international ambition by promoting Dutch Health Design.

First date of publication: October 21, 2016

SPCBZZ O

GIVING CHILDREN THE ASTRONAUT'S
VIEW OF PLANET EARTH.

Thanks to
Petra van Dijk, MindLabs

The development of MindLabs in Tilburg

Most exciting innovations appear in cross-overs between disciplines. In the city of Tilburg (the 6th largest city in the southern part of the Netherlands), a new regional initiative 'MindLabs'[13] was announced in 2016 and started in the summer of 2017. Tilburg works on the development of an ecosystem where knowledge institutes, public and private organizations, start-ups and scale-ups collaborate with a focus on interactive technologies and behavior.

In the past century, the Tilburg economy has to a large extent been based upon textile production. After the industrialization, a period of unemployment started, followed by a slow shift towards a knowledge economy. Nowadays a textile museum remembers to the rich textile history. At the same time, this history is still alive as fashion, being part of creative industries, is a very innovative sector. Smart textiles know many different applications already. Think of incubator babies wearing an outfit with integrated sensors that can measure respiration, heart rate, and so on.

Over the past years, Tilburgs' knowledge institutes have developed their own specific research and educational programs in relation to creative industries. For instance, Fontys University of Applied Sciences includes an academy for creative industries, next to schools for ICT and Journalism. The recent initiative 'MindLabs' was launched with the collective ambition to create a unique ecosystem where education, research, and business reinforce each other on the crossings of interactive technologies and behavior.

The vision behind this initiative is that digitalization is the key driver for the transition of our society and economy. These changes require new educational programs, new research methodologies (think of design research, co-creation, embedded research, and living labs), and new and flexible business models. Virtual- and augmented reality, language technologies, robotics and avatars, and gamification are important themes in the development of MindLabs. Application domains are manyfold, ranging from health and well-being to smart industry.

June 2016, Tilburg University, Fontys University of Applied Sciences, the regional education center ROC Tilburg, and the municipality of Tilburg signed a letter of intent for collaboration. The Persgroep (a large Dutch-Flemish publisher with both national and regional newspapers, as well as a strong online outreach with diverse websites and radio) has joined the consortium as a first private partner and other private partners have shown serious interest. The coming years will have to prove the potential of MindLabs as an iconic hotspot.

First date of publication: January 24, 2018

The State of Fashion and creative city Arnhem

Context
Creative industries policies have stimulated regional creative hot spots, next to specific creative sectors such as fashion (design). At a national level, creative industries has been appointed one of the nine Dutch topsectors. Each topsector in the Netherlands focusses on human capital development, internationalization, and knowledge and innovation.

Concerning knowledge and innovation, six networks have been stimulated by the national topsector Creative Industries over the past years. Next Fashion was one of these national networks, with support of the city of Arnhem, as well as the province of Gelderland in the Eastern part of the Netherlands.

Creative City Arnhem

Arnhem has transformed into a creative city for several years already, with a growing number of creative start-ups and an applied university for the arts, 'ArtEZ'. ArtEZ hosts one of the three Dutch centers of expertise on creative industries called 'Futuremakers'. Researchers work together with public- and private organizations in research projects. The aim is *"to develop more sustainable value chains for products and services in the field of fashion, textiles, product and interior design".*[14]

Education, production, and presentation are all represented in the creative chain of Arnhem. Hence, the city can further develop her cultural and creative sector consisting of arts, music, dance, design, and fashion. Creative industries play an important role in innovation and new jobs. Arnhem is one of the top three cities in the Netherlands related to creative industries employment.[15]

Arnhem has also joined forces with the city Nijmegen in cultural policies and activities. In this way a stronger national position can be realized. Furthermore, the current collaboration in the applied university Arnhem-Nijmegen (HAN) can be further extended between the two cities.

Fashion and Design Festival

Every year in June, Arnhem organizes the Fashion + Design festival with exhibitions, fashion shows, performances, and events throughout the city. The 'State of Fashion 2018: searching for the new luxury' exhibition was part of this festival. The 2018 edition is about sustainable solutions in the use of materials, in production, as well as in the consumption of fashion.[16]

"State of Fashion 2018 – searching for the new luxury explores a new sense of conscious consumerism, by embracing state-of-the-art technologies, innovative production methods and ingenious business models, and by exploring the exiting area in which science and fashion design meet." (Jose Teunissen, curator)[17]

Concluding, the cultural and creative sector in Arnhem already has a strong foothold, as well as good perspectives. In the coming years, further collaboration, both at a regional and national level, is important in order to continue to build upon the current position. The city of Arnhem has a responsibility to maintain their support in enabling growth in this promising sector.

First date of publication: June 26, 2018

International good practices

A range of international good practices in cultural and creative industries practice and policy making is described and illustrated. Examples from Russia, Kazachstan, Israel, and the Middle East are discussed.

Unknown territories: creative industries in Russia

Who is not familiar with the Russian opera or the Hermitage? Russia has some great history and treasures in cultural and creative industries. But Russia also knows some real challenges, such as intellectual property rights (IPR) in relation to cultural and creative sectors. Over the past years, however, Russia is opening up and showing a growing cultural and creative sector.

Russia
In 2009, an analysis was made of cultural industries in Russia by the Helsinki School of Economics.[18] In this report, creative industries are divided into traditional culture, entertainment sector, film industry, games industry, and cultural tourism. In addition, the analysis discerns between governmental, non-governmental and commercial organizations in Russia's cultural industries.

From the analysis a dual picture emerged. On the one hand, the political structure is relevant as creative industries have not been recognized in national policies or legislation yet. IPR protection is still weak and foreign investments are limited. On the other hand, Russia knows a strong cultural heritage. Especially in the big cities young Russians have a global lifestyle, and education and science have a strong basis. Almost ten years later, the climate for creativity and innovation is slowly changing.

Autumn 2017, the Analytical Center for Government of the Russian Federation published an article on the growth potential of the creative industry in Russia.[19] In this bulletin on education, the creative industry is seen as *"becoming one of the most important areas of economic and social development"*, in relation to *"this period of science and technology transformations, mass digitalization, and the increasing role of intellectual property"*. The role of education is believed to be of high relevance with regard to the demands of the labor market: *"At the moment (17 October 2017) the creative industry is estimated 0,5% of the GDP, but by 2025 its share may increase several-fold."*[20]

Creative cities
Saint Petersburg is widely recognized for it's outstanding arts infrastructure with the Hermitage as worldfamous landmark. Many initiatives have been launched over the past years. At the Higher School of Economics in Saint Petersburg, cultural and creative industries courses are taught.[21] Furthermore, international collaboration, such as with the UK and Finland, helps in the development of the cultural and creative industries sector.

Moscow is a vibrant metropolis where creative industry initiatives have arisen over the past years, ranging from cultural and creative clusters to dedicated programmes. Several cultural and creative spaces have opened, programs have been initiated such as START (for visual arts), as well as institutes such as Strelka geared at media, architecture, and design.[22]

Conclusions

Research, education, and entrepreneurship are three basic pillars in economic development, also for creative industries. Local and national governments can play an important role in stimulating this sector as well as enabling growth by creating the right conditions, for instance related to IPR. The cultural and creative industries sector in Russia has real potential. Will a giant wake up the coming years?

First date of publication: August 20, 2018

Creative industries in the Middle East

Middle East and CCS

According to CISAC[23], Africa and the Middle East are a rising market for the Cultural and Creative Sectors (CCS) with 58 billion US dollar in revenues (3% of worldwide CCS) and 2.4 million jobs (8% of worldwide CCS), according to EY (December 2015).[24] In the CISAC comparison of CCS in worldwide regions, the growth seems to be high in the Middle East. In 2017, the World Bank estimated *"creative industries are growing fastest at more than 10% a year"*[25] in the Middle-East.

Numbers differ though for specific countries, as well as for the characteristics of the CCS vary from TV to games, and from architecture to visual arts. The World Bank estimates creative industries to contribute 7% to the global GDP in Kuwait. CCS in other Middle East countries, such as the United Arab Emirates, are rising very fast.[26]

Some countries have strong investment programs based on cultural and creative industries policy. Beginning of 2018, the United Arab Emirates launched the UAE Cultural Development Fund, related to the Ministry of Culture and Knowledge Development.[27] In this way, cultural activities and projects can be effectively supported.

When comparing growth numbers between countries and regions, the definition of cultural and creative industries remains relevant. Further, characteristics related to Florida's Talent, Tolerance and Technology[28], differ strongly for each country. Finally, successful policy making is not easily being copied. Every country has it's own natural strenghts and specific opportunities.

Creative industries examples

UAE

The two major creative cities in the United Arab Emirates are Dubai and Abu Dhabi. Dubai hosts the largest skyscraper in the world, the Burj Al Khalifa. Furthermore, one can ski in a large shopping mall, where pinguins recide (in the middle of the desert)! Architecture, design, fashion, and arts are well represented creative sectors. In Abu Dhabi, the auxiliary branche of the French Louvre museum is an astonishing architectural icon. Additionally Abu Dhabi hosts the Ferrari World theme park and also a Warner Bross studio next to the Yas Marina race circuit: a true experience economy.

Until 1958, no oil was found yet as a major vehicle behind this economic growth and prosperity. From that perspective, one could debate about what a creative economy looks like, both superficial (e.g. the Louvre museum), but also under the surface (the fundamentals of creativity). At the same time the Middle Eastern United Arab Emirates are relatively tolerant. The UAE make use of the newest technologies and give room for talent with the development of private higher educational institutes that collaborate with other international universities, as well as large multinational companies.

Jordan

In the Jordan Times (June 2015), creative industries potential was highlighted: *"Focusing on creative industries will help attract tourists and promote the country."*[29] Jordan is slowly opening up for new economic sectors, such as the creative industries. Deserts and the ancient city of Petra have been extensively used as a film set, but other cultural or creative sectors seem to be underdeveloped thus far. In contrast to the UAE, giving a strong impuls to the creative industries by way of funding is a challenge in Jordan.

Conclusions

The Middle East region has a lot of potential for CCS, although the potential differs for each country. The worldwide share in CCS is still limited, but fast growing. Governments play an important role in stimulating CCS. The next challenge would be to combine creative industries strenght in developing solutions for other sectors, such as mobility, healthcare, and so on.

First date of publication: October 30, 2018

Israel as a good practice for creative start-ups

Innovative Israel
In 2009, Dan Senor and Saul Singer published their book 'Start-up Nation: The Story of Israel's Economic Miracle'. The authors raise and answer the question why Israel, a young and small country with hardly any natural resources and surrounded by enemies, has more start-ups than large and peaceful countries like Japan, China, India, or Canada.

Other sources confirm this trend, pointing at a mix of talent, research universities, and venture capital: *"at the start of 2009, some 63 Israeli companies were listed on the NASDAQ, more than those of any other foreign country."*[30]

Start-up climate
With a population of 8,5 million inhabitants, this young country has successfully launched many new (technology) start-ups over

the past decades. Further, Israel has attracted many foreign investors, especially in domains such as agritech, cybersecurity, digital health, fintech, watertech and industry 4.0.[31]

Most Israeli's have a progressive attitude, which is partly due to the continuous threat of war since 70 years of the independent state of Israel. As a result of this situation, the army makes enormous investments in (technology-driven) innovation.

This is not unique. For instance in the United States, research and development for anti-malaria tablets was not commercially attractive for a long time. However, it became urgent and thus necessary for the army as more soldiers were killed by malaria than bullets in the Vietnam war. Another example is the Internet, that primarily started as an army invention.

Other characteristics of the strong start-up culture have been an attractive tax climate and the entrepreneurial spirit of Israeli's. Whether Israel or Tel Aviv region will become a next Silicon Valley, or 'Silicon Wadi', is questionable. In Israel the possibilities for upscaling are limited.[32] International investors, though, have serious interest in these start-ups.

Creative city Tel Aviv
Jerusalem and Tel Aviv have previously been described as true opposites: ying and yang. Where Jerusalem is the religious and more conservative city, Tel Aviv is vibrant and progressive. Richard Florida indicated Talent, Tolerance, and Technology as conditions for a strong creative class. These three T's are fully met in the city of Tel Aviv.

Tel Aviv, situated on the Mediteranean coastline, has a mixed population, a strong gay community, an extensive nightlife, many events and festivals, and a dynamic cultural and creative sector.

Design, (media) arts, fashion, and architecture (Bauhaus) are prominent in Tel Aviv. In combination with a strong tech culture and research universities, this is an ideal area for creatives.

Creative start-ups
The Israel organization 'Start-up nation central' has supported the Creative Business Cup competition for several years already. Creative industries are known for their long tail of small- and medium-sized companies. Innovation is in the DNA of the creative class.

> **CREATIVE BUSINESS CUP**[33]
> *"Creative Business Cup is a global year-round initiative that empowers entrepreneurs in the creative industries, helping them grow their business ideas, connecting them to investors and the global markets, and strengthening their innovative capabilities to the benefit of industry and society."*

The strenght of creative industries could be to provide solutions for societal challenges, as prioritized by the organization 'start-up nation central': Agritech, Cybersecurity, Digital Health, Fintech, Watertech and Industry 4.0. As a result, cultural and creative sectors might realize valuable cross-overs in the near future.

First date of publication: November 5, 2018

Creative industries in Kazakhstan:
Artificial Imagination?

In 1991, Kazakhstan in central Asia became independent of the former USSR. Since that time, the 8th largest country in the world rapidly developed. In 1997 the former capital city Alma Aty was replaced by Astana, a new-designed city. This has resulted in a futuristic skyline designed by international architects.

Being the 17th largest oil producer in the world makes the economy of Kazakhstan strongly rely on oil and gas resources. Only after 1990 the former Soviet state-run economy could start moving towards a market economy. However, these changes have taken a lot of time. Kazakhstan slowly opened up to the wider region, for instance by joining the Eurasiatic Economic Union in 2015.

Further, investments in the infrastructure have boosted the economy. The new Silk Road for instance, initiated by China's President Xi Jinping, connects China with Europe via Kazakhstan's cities Alma Aty and Astana. Astana's infrastructure received another boost by hosting and organizing the World Expo in 2017.

From June 10 – September 10, 2017, Astana was host of the World Expo. Within 3 months, almost 4 million people visited the World Expo. The Netherlands pavilion was designed by Hypsos, stressing the Dutch creative mindset in relation to future energy challenges.

In the context of the World Expo 2017, the Astana Contemporary Art Center organized an interesting exhibition about 'Artists & Robots'. This exhibition showed 17 installations, products of artificial intelligence, fuelled by pioneering artists, ranging from pictures and sculptures to architecture, design, and music.

This development where machines or robots are not only intelligent, but also creative, raises questions about the boundaries of art. Discussions started about whether machines are really 'creative' or that they just incrementally learn and build on existing ideas, in contrast to humans who can create new concepts and structures.

ARTISTS & ROBOTS[34]
"The Age of Artificial Imagination: Could a machine do what an artist does? Could a robot replace a painter or a sculpture? To what degree can we talk about artificial creativity?"

Creative industries should embrace these (digital) developments, in order to remain relevant and to be able to anticipate on future challenges. Digitalization of our society won't stop and the message is to experiment and find (or reinvent) your role as a creative.

Concerning Astana, the creation of this 'artificial city' is a fascinating product of creative industries in terms of design and architecture. Instead of buiding upon existing structures, a brand new city was developed. The question is whether Astana and Kazachstan will be able to continue building on this future perspective, which is still very dependant on oil and gas incomes today. Maybe 'Artificial Imagination' can help shape the future?

First date of publication: October 25, 2017

Outreach and dissemination

In this section, outreach and dissemination are discussed and illustrated with three cases: the European Creative Industries Festival 'MeConvention' in Stockholm, the European Creative Industries Summit in Vienna functioning as an important platform, and Sri Lanka's Design Festival.

Innovative Stockholm and the MeConvention

Stockholm creative city
The cultural and creative industries in Sweden enjoy a prosperous climate with Stockholm as their vibrant capital city. In 2010, the Swedish Council for Cultural and Creative Industries was founded in order to stimulate cultural and creative industries.[35] Stockholm has a strong cultural basis with many museums and art centers. In addition, the city has a lively start-up scene. A nice example is the network and co-working space the Impact Hub[36], representing part of a global network of social entrepreneurs.

Stockholm tech city
Digitalization is the key driver of tomorrow's innovations. In the beginning of September 2018, Stockholm organized the STHLM Tech Fest.[37] Stockholm hosts many tech companies like IBM and Google, but also many tech start-ups. Next to the

impact of technology, such as virtual reality, robotics, and the
'Internet of Things', topics in the STHLM Fest were the application of technology in domains such as food, security, retail, and
banking.

MeConvention
During that same week in the beginning of September 2018,
Stockholm also hosted the creative conference MeConvention.
MeConvention is a daughter event of the yearly South By South-
west creative festival in Austin, Texas.[38] The MeConvention 2018
in Stockholm was the second European edition.

> **MECONVENTION**[39]
> *"The MeConvention, a unique conference and festival event, aims to connect*
> *bright minds across all industries in order to shape the future. A collaboration*
> *between Mercedes-Benz and SXSW, the first me Convention was held in 2017 at*
> *the International Motor Show (IAA) in Frankfurt, Germany. As proven leaders in*
> *innovation and leadership, Mercedes-Benz and SXSW bring together global leaders*
> *and pioneers across art, music, technology, science and more, to inspire unique*
> *conversations and the exchange of knowledge."*

The three days of inspiration started with an exploration day
throughout the city with art and architecture, a 'tech start-up
safari', and meeting of organizations that facilitate start-ups
such as the Founder Institute. Stockholm also has a growing
makerspace, with amongst others a biohacking lab, featuring
'The Future of Citizen Tech'. The photograph museum served
as a great evening spot with beautiful views on the old town.

During the two conference days at 'Nacka Strandmässon', a former car factory, many interesting topics were explored, often at
the crossings of technology, creativity, and societal challenges.
For instance: blockchain solutions to save the ocean,

developments in policy making concerning killer robots, and digital human rights.

One of the criteria for success of international conferences is a strong mix of topics presented in creative formats. Further, successful conferences need icons, such as the Swedish co-founder of Abba, Björn Ulvaeus, who discussed how to stay ahead in today's music industries.

Conclusions
Just like South By Southwest, MeConvention combines the innovative power of new technologies and digitalization with creativity. Stockholm proves to be a great place for innovation with a rich start-up climate and it has created a strong basis to remain one of the leading start-up cities in the world.

First date of publication: September 12, 2018

European Creative Industries Summit in Austria

According to the Economist Intelligence Unit, Vienna ranks
highest (with a 99,1% score, elected out of 140 cities) on the
Global Liveability Index 2018.[40] No surprise that over 40% of the
Austrian creatives work in Vienna. With over 40.000 creative
enterprises and over 150.000 jobs, creative industries in Austria
contribute about euro 8,6 billion gross value at factor costs,
which is equivalent to 3,9% of the overall economy.[41] Creative
industries represent a highly relevant and growing part of the
Austrian economy.

In their seventh Austrian Creative Industries Report, Kreativwirtschaft Austria provides insight not only in creative industries as
such, but also in the effect of creative industries on the national
economy, on the Austrian market, on investments and exports,
on innovation, and on businesses: *"Any one euro of value added in*

the creative industries produces another 0,76 euros in the rest of the economy".

Vienna Design Week
From September, 28 to October 7, 2018, the 12th edition of the Vienna Design Week took place. Vienna hosts an interesting design culture. The design week represents an international platform to highlight different kinds of design production, varying from products and services to environments and experiences. One of the locations was the former 'Socialmedizinisches Zentrum Sophienspital' with different design exhibitions and VR-based experiences.

VIENNA DESIGN WEEK[42]

"Vienna Design Week is Austria´s largest design festival, with a variety of locations and events in Vienna. The festival, curated by Lilli Hollein entered its 12th round this year. Opening up creative processes and giving scope for experimentation on site are core elements of the festival concept.

During Vienna Design Week, the city becomes a platform and showcase of design. Design is more than just a designed object. Vienna Design Week defines design as an essential part of the cultural production. The festival shows that design shapes our material culture, our every-day life and our world as consumers. Simultaneously, it influences our lifestyles and most fundamentally our aesthetic senses and judgements."

ECIS 2018 summit
The European Creative Industries Summit (ECIS) 2018, the 8th edition already, was organized from October 3-4 during the Vienna Design Week by the European Creative Business Network (ECBN). The summit took place at the Austrian Federal Economic Chamber in Vienna, during the Austrian EU Presidency.

Speeches from the eurocommissioner Tibor Navracsics, the Austrian Federal Minister of Digital and Economic Affairs Margarete Schramböck, and Member of the European Parliament and co-chair of the intergroup for Creative Industries Christian Ehler addressed global challenges demanding for an innovative and creative Europe.

During the Summit, eight groups worked on cross-over challenges for cultural and creative industries and came up with concrete proposals for future policy making.

Lobby European Research Framework Program
May 2018, Frits Grotenhuis and Bernd Fesel already wrote an argumentation to mainstream benefits for the cultural and creative sectors.[43] The 8th European Research Framework Program Horizon 2020 had a strong focus on grand societal challenges. However, at that time there was no room for cross-overs between disciplines.

The cultural and creative sectors can be strong players in cross-over innovations. During ECIS 2018, preliminary announcements were made about plans to create funds for cross-innovation and cultural and creative industries in the next research framework program. The coming months will show whether cross-innovation and cultural and creative sectors have become recognized as drivers for Europe's future.

First date of publication: October 16, 2018

Creative Sri Lanka: hot spot in South Asia

Background

Sri Lanka, tropical island in the Indian ocean with around 22 million inhabitants, has a relatively modern industrial economy. Textile and fashion have been important pillars until today. The challenge is to transform to a global economy that is ready for the 21st century. Sri Lanka wants to be the catalyst for the South Asia region and has a lot of potential.

Partly due to investments from China, the infrastructure in Sri Lanka is solid with a new harbor and airpor in the southern part of Sri Lanka. These investments are part of China's new silk route ambition.[44] Todays political situation is unstable and insecure for investors with new elections in the beginning of 2019.

Areas where Sri Lanka's economy could benefit are creative industries and digitalization. Creative industries' sectors like design and fashion are natural strenghts of the country's economy. With regard to digitalization, Sri Lanka develops ICT software and hardware industries, but also ICT (cloud-based) services. These sectors can reinforce each other, think of the Virtual Fitting Room of the company SenseMe.[45]

Sri Lanka's creative industries is diverse, although fashion and design are most prevalent. Textiles have been an important export product. One of the large textile companies in Sri Lanka is Star Textile Processing Industries[46], where the usage of new technologies becomes more and more important. Another interesting company is the Hirdaramani Mihila factory[47], *"Asia's FIRST Carbon Neutral Apparel Manufacturer and the county's iconic green factory."*[48]

Academy of Design
The Academy of Design (AOD)[49], as a private higher educational institute, is an important organization and driver for Sri Lanka's creative industries ambition. The AOD closely collaborates with partners, such as the Northumbria University in the UK, in programs about fashion, design, arts, architecture and built environment, and more.

The AOD has been an engine behind important design initiatives in Sri Lanka, such as the Island Craft Project, the Fashion Market, and the Sri Lanks Design Festival. With education and exposure, the AOD creates opportunities both for students, professionals, and businesses to achieve their ambitions in creative industries.

Furthermore, the AOD is developing a new location where new forms of education can be experimented with, but it will also provide modern meeting places, host future working places, and even serve as an incubator. In this way, the sector will have a strong basis for future growth.

Sri Lanka Design Festival 2018
November 2018, the yearly Sri Lanka Design Week (SLDF)[50] was held for the 8th time. The previous month, October 2018, the Mercedes Benz fashion week[51] was organized. These platforms have an important function to showcase the newest developments in (potential) products and services, but they also provide an opportunity for students, small businesses, and (potential) customers and investors to meet and exchange.

Collaboration with large companies such as Mercedes Benz is becoming a trend. Next to Sri Lanka, Mercedes Benz sponsors and collaborates in fashion weeks in Australia, Istanbul, Amsterdam, and many other cities. Mercedes Benz was also main sponsor of the European creative event MeConvention in Stockholm (September 2018).

Delegations from the United Kingdom and the Netherlands participated in the 2018 edition of SLDF. In the Creative Economies Policy Forum, which was hosted by the British Council in partnership with the AOD and the Sri Lanka Design Festival, a core working group for Sri Lanka's creative economy was established.

The Dutch delegation organized workshops and roundtables to exchange good practices in the development of creative industries. Students and alumni from the AOD showcased their work at Trace Expert City, an innovative center in the heart of Colombo.

Towards a national policy strategy
Building upon the previous success, network, and organization, Sri Lanka is ready for a next leap. The first blueprints were built by the AOD in collaboration with the British Council. During the Sri Lanka Design Festival, international partners gathered and

discussed a future national policy strategy for Sri Lanka's creative industries.

This development has mainly been driven by private organizations. Long-term success will be found in the collaboration between education- and knowledge institutes, businesses, and public bodies. Important public bodies can be ministries, but also the Expert Development Board, and Chamber of Commerce.

Like in many other countries, creative industries development starts with creating awareness and recognition of the (potential of the) sector. In developing countries, creative industries are often perceived as 'luxury' and very insecure for economic prosperity, both at a micro and macro level. Sri Lanka, however, is at the threshold of a new era in her economic development. The coming years will show whether parties have been able to create synergy and realization of the potential.

First date of publication: November 22, 2018

Alternative perspectives

This section illustrates a diversity of fields where cultural and creative industries can play a significant role and add value: effective altruism, behavioral change, the role of musea, and future education.

Creative industries and effective altruism

Nowadays creative industries are often viewed from an economic perspective: what is the economic value of creative industries? Next to economic value, societal value may be even more important. Think about the 3P's (People, Planet, and Profit): there is more than just economic benefit.

An American movement that recently arrived in Europe focuses on 'effective altruism'[52]. Peter Singer argues in his book 'The most good you can do' (2015) that many 'good' is not effective at all, though often based on good feeling or emotions. But how efficient and effective are these good intentions and projects in fact? Effective altruism is about how we can use our resources the most to help others. Based on evidence and analysis effective altruists work on the 'very best causes'.

Creative industries have potential to enable effective altruism projects, with design, architecture, (smart) fashion, gamification, and so on.

Most of the creative industries contributions can be called cross-over (pilot) projects, where different disciplines come together.

One example is the floating pavilion in Rotterdam, the Netherlands, where three floating domes are connected with a floating square.[53] The aim of this project is to develop and test floating buildings in relation to climate-resistant urbanisation on the water. Another example is the fairphone project by the Amsterdam-based organization Waag Society, with the aim to develop a smart phone that is both fair and sustainable.[54] By redesigning the system, the different required components can be collected, assembled and possibly recycled in a fair way. A third example is the 'emergency sanitation operating system', abbreviated eSOS.[55] Hygenic sanitation should be a basic condition for all people, also those living in remote or poor rural areas. In developing countries and in disaster areas (think about an earthquake or flood), the risk of bacteria and viruses is very high. With the help of integrated sensors the eSOS smart toilet measures and monitors the ratio of urine and faeces on malnourishment or dehydration.

Since 2011 the Amsterdam-based platform 'What Design Can Do' organizes a yearly conference about the power of design.[56] This platform also organizes the 'What Design Can Do Challenge'. The previous edition focused on solutions for refugees. One of the solutions, jointly developed with the IKEA foundation, was the 'better shelter': a small light-weight modular house with solar panels. Another solution was the 'Centifloat', a smart floating boat that can be inflated within 3 minutes and has over 60 grab handles preventing people who can not swim from drowning. In 2017 the design challenge concerns climate change.

Another recent research project and exhibition in Tel Aviv, Israel, is called '3.5 Square Meters: Constructive Responses to Natural Disasters'.[57] In this publication and exhibition several projects illustrated the power of creative industries in relation to solutions for natural disasters. Examples are related to social technologies (e.g. the Airbnb Global Disaster Response & Relief Program for people who lost their homes), DIY projects such as the 'better shelter' (see the same example above with the IKEA foundation and UNHCR), storytelling and sharing knowledge (e.g. the Japanese wiki-like platform OLIVE where tips and tutorials for refugees are being shared).

Concluding, the classic boundary between economic- and societal value should be broken down: economic benefit follows societal relevance. Applying effective altruism to creative industries could be a challenging but rewarding mission!

First date of publication: May 15, 2017

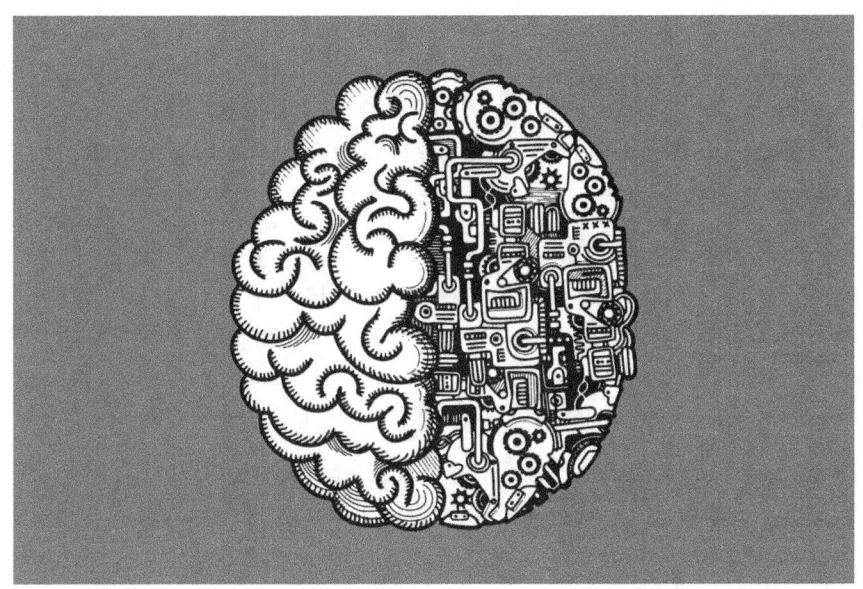

Creative industries and behavioral change

The area of brain, cognition, and behavior is upcoming and highly relevant to creative industries. In the design of new processes, products, and services, we often design for 'preferred behavior'. Application areas are manyfold, varying from healthy living and de-escalating agressive behavior, to airports and shopping malls.

Think for instance about the design of an airport where logistic throughput of passengers is key. Amsterdam Schiphol airport is a strong example of Dutch design where the routing of the constantly growing number of passengers seems to be fully natural. People are being efficiently 'guided' through the process of check-in, passport control and boarding the aircraft.

Another example is the use of light in (care) environments where evidence has been found that agressive behavior of patients could be diminished. Another project using the effects of light is in the inner-city center of Eindhoven where is being experimented with mechanisms for de-escalation of aggressive behavior in the entertainment area 'Stratumseind' at night.[58] For instance, arousal levels may lower and self-control enhanced through the utilization of interactive light.

In shopping environments experiments with music, light, temperature, and other conditions try to unraffle how to maximize the time (and money) that people spend. In this respect, new fields such as neuromarketing flourish based upon new insights on (perceived) consumer preferences.

With regard to a healthy lifestyle, big data becomes key to discern specific patterns of behavior in relation to different contexts as well as tailorized advise to individuals: how to design for personalized health? Self management becomes more important and convenient with the help of the 'quantified self' movement based upon your own data generation.

E-coaching is a promising area, where new insights should further optimize personal feedback. However, until today, designing for behavior doesn't prove to be an easy endavor. What makes it that some people more or less easily stick to health habits, while others don't? How to support people to adopt a healthier lifestyle in the longer run?

Games, as part of the broad scope of creative industries, are often used in measuring or influencing behavior. Several research projects with topics such as how to measure effective executive functioning of children with ADHD, or how to (virtually) coach people with a post-traumatic stress disorder, have been funded.

Knowledge about neurosciences contributes to effective strategies and policy making in supporting and changing specific behavior. As illustrated with the examples in this blog, creative industries can play an important role in this area. Based on the existing and growing evidence on effective interventions, the potential for creative industries is both relevant and substantial.

First date of publication: April 7, 2017

Creative industries and future education

Discussions about future education are trending. So-called 21st century skills, lifelong learning, living labs, digital education, MOOCs, microcredentials, and blockchain certificates are some typical buzzwords. Students of today are digital natives and make fully use of the wide array of digital possibilities. These students demand freedom of choice of content (what), time (when), and place (where) in education.

At the same time, many teachers can hardly follow these digital natives. As a result, demand and supply of education do not match anymore. Educational 'supply' in terms of elementary schools, secondary education, and higher educational institutes has slowly become aware of the need for change. 'Demand' in terms of both the students as well as the labor market (possible employers) is changing really fast.

Next to knowledge, specific characteristics such as creativity, multidisciplinarity, team collaboration, and 'character' have become requirements for a successful career. Neumeijer argues in his book 'Metaskills: Five Talents for the Robotic Age'[59] that we need the following skills in order to be successful professionals: feeling (intuition and empathy), seeing (systems thinking), dreaming (applied imagination), making (design), and learning (autodidacts).

In the Netherlands, the Dutch topsectors have developed so-called human capital agendas in order to prepare today's talents for the labor market of tomorrow. Based on 20 pilot projects, the Dutch topsectors recently advised the government to build (upon) learning communities where study, work and innovation come together. Interestingly enough this looks like the former master-apprentice relationship developed during the middle ages, which still proves to be relevant.

Further, the Dutch universities developed a joint research agenda on digital society with a focus on societal challenges, including learning and education: how to enable people to participate meaningfully in all stages of life? Creative industries could play an important role in this perspective.

Creative industries already experiment and work for many years in living labs; creatives make use of co-design, user-centered design, gamification principles, and design thinking as an alternative approach for learning, collaboration, and problem solving. New (creative) technologies, such as virtual- and augmented reality, give a boost to future learning. Concluding, creative industries should actively take her role in the design and further development of future education.

First date of publication: March 12, 2018

Museums adrift in the 21ˢᵗ century

Museums have witnessed an enormous transformation over the past decennia. *"During the past twenty years, more art museums have been built than in the previous centuries."*[60] From an international perspective it becomes clear that the role of musea is changing. More and more, musea have a public function, showcasing societal themes in an interactive manner.

Next to new constructions, more often former industrial buildings are revitalized with a museum function. In Liverpool (United Kingdom), the Beatles museum is located in the former docks. This museum, despite its location, is organized in a very old-fashioned way, sequential and passive (tourist follow each other with a headset from the one room to the other). The EPIC museum about the emigration history in Dublin (Ireland) is also located in the former docks, but is very modern and interactive with a great user-experience. This museum was also proclaimed as *"Europe's leading tourist attraction 2019"*.[61]

Next to revitalizing old buildings, more iconic buildings are developed of which some are real treasures of architecture. In Western Europe examples are the 'Museum aan de Stroom' (MAS) in Antwerp (Belgium), the Guggenheim in Bilbao (Spain), but also the film museum Eye in Amsterdam (the Netherlands). Also in other parts of the world, such as the Middle East, beautiful musea have been built. The National Museum of Quatar is one of these examples, designed by western architects.

From borrowing art to predatory art
Some years ago, in Abu Dhabu, an icon of design and architecture was developed as auxiliary branch of the Louvre museum in Paris (France). The question arises to what extent can a museum have an original collection in relation to her own art productions, acquired art, and borrowing art? What does this imply for the cultural climate and the user experience of visitors, but also for inhabitents? Anyway, the Abu Dhabi Louvre registered over a million visitors in the first year of opening![62]

Next to borrowing art, predatory art is a recent (political) topic, especially for older museums showcasing history in relation to a colonial background. What is predatory art and how to deal with this as a nation? This is like hitting an open nerve for nations that were former colonies as well as the colonizing nations, such as the slavery history of the Netherlands in Surinam. The past years both the Dutch Tropenmuseum (museum of world cultures) and Dutch Rijksmuseum (museum of Dutch art and history) have announced to return predatory art to the formerly colonized countries.[63]

An interesting example or paradox can be found in the United Kingdom. The Liverpool slavery museum fully recognizes the dark ages of slavery as a colonizing country (the former British empire). Only a few hundred kilometres away in London, in the British museum, a rather different perspective is chosen in relation to predatory art. The British Museum explains how half of the so-called 'Parthenon sculptures' (as parts of the famous tempel at the Akropolis mountain in Athens) have arrived in the United Kingdom.[64] The former envoy of the British Crown, Elgin, is held responsible.

Although the Greek government since the eighties (so far in vain) requested to bring the Parthenon sculptures back to Athens, the British museum does not seem to have intentions to do so: *"Elgins's removal of the sculptures from the ruins of the building has always been a matter for discussion, but one thing is certain – his actions spared them further damage by vandalism, weathering and pollution. It is also thanks to Elgin that generations of visitors have been able to see the sculptures at eye level rather than high up on the building."*[65]

The future of museums
In short, museums are adrift. Museums reflect on their role in society and experiment with new ways to create unique user experiences. Nowadays supported by new technologies such as virtual reality they try to attract sufficient visitors. New museums are often located at industrial heritage sites or in iconic new buildings. Both old and new museums focus their collections on societal challenges ranging from climate to safety, or from immigration to an inclusive society.

Eindhoven (the Netherlands) inventorizes the feasibility of a Rijks-museum for design.[66] The ambition is to develop a museum aimed at (projections of) the future, compared to other museums in the southern part of the Netherlands. The success of the museum will depend on a combination of the location, the unique character of the museum in the region, the perceived visitor experience and -interaction, next to the role of design in developing solutions for societal challenges.

First date of publication: September 17, 2019

Future perspectives

In this section, future perspectives are envisioned. A previous lookout with trends for 2017 still seems to be highly relevant. Furthermore, a strong plea for European cultural and creative industries funding as an important driver for innovation is made. The section ends with future directions for cultural and creative industries after the corona crisis.

Trends in cultural and creative industries

What will be the impact of digitalization on creative industries? How to deal with exclusion, fading away the middle class, and being driven by the creative class? These two trends have been discussed in a blog end of 2016 as a forecast of 2017, but still seem to be highly relevant today.

A brief perspective over the past years: creative industries, especially from a policy perspective, have for a long period of time been viewed as a strong mixture of culture and economy. The direct economic contribution to the gross net product of the Netherlands counts for about 2-3% for years already. Of course this may vary between countries and regions and will depend on the definition that is being used, but the statistics are relatively stable. However, the growth potential is in the indirect value of creative industries to other societal and economic sectors such as healthcare or mobility (the so-called cross-overs). Nowadays, many projects are experimenting with these cross-overs in order to create value. Looking forward to 2017 and beyond, two major trends will have a strong impact on creative industries in the coming years.

1. Digitalization

The exponential growth of data, the further integration of technologies, and the 'Internet of Things' have a strong impact on (the role of) creative industries. Digitalization has already shown to be a very disruptive development. Think about the growing internet-based platforms, game changers that demand a transformation of business models in current sectors. This does not only have impact on some familiar examples such as the taxi sector with Uber or the hotel sector with Airbnb. The coming years, about every sector will have to adjust, ranging from energy to retail, and from education to safety. In 2016 virtual- and augmented reality really (who has not played Pokemon Go?) came through to a large audience. In 2017, these developments will continue even at a faster pace, as more and more technologies become integrated.

What does this imply for creative industries? Think about the role of design in (social) robotics in relation to elderly care. How to increase the acceptance and adoption of new technologies for consumers, what would be relevant conditions? Other examples are the developments in language technologies in relation to the exponential growth of big data: think about new forms of journalism, fact checking, and the influence of social media on the recent elections in the USA. With the help of big data, personalization of the needs of the individual consumer becomes more accurate every day, even predicting your needs of tomorrow.

Think about applications in retail (internet shopping) where 'supply creates demand', based on personalized profiles.

2. Exclusion

Richard Florida, author of the bestseller 'The rise of the creative class' in 2002[67], will publish a new book in the beginning of 2017: 'The new urban crisis'.[68] This book deals with the downsides of creative industries development. After decades of prosperous growth and a positive attitude towards the creative class, we now become aware of the downsides. According to Florida, gentrification, segregation and inequality have taken a rise, following the previous rise of the creative class. Exclusion is a growing phenomenon: middle class people cannot or hardly afford to buy a house in creative cities. Political discussions about the declining middle class in society are certainly appropriate for creative cities. Only the upper class and successful companies can afford to reside in these expensive city centers.

Creative industries as a grown-up sector needs to better understand such processes and find suitable solutions for these challenges. The Netherlands Organization for Scientific Research will run a creative industries call in 2017, geared at innovative research projects on 'technological, economic and cultural transformation of the city'. This is an important first step to gain thorough knowledge on the one hand and to experiment with redesigning the cities of the future on the other. Another illustration is the PhD study of Jeanette Nijkamp, published in 2016, about the effect of the creative class in two neighborhoods in the city of Rotterdam, the Netherlands 'Counting on Creativity. The Creative Class as Antidote for Neighborhood Decline: the case of Rotterdam.'[69] Nijkamp found that only presence of the creative class does not necessarily result into more economic growth or a flourishing neighborhood. Further, social improvement of neighborhoods was difficult to measure and thus to prove.

Concluding, the coming period will be challenging for creative industries with regard to digitalization and exclusion. Let the creative class prove her value by redesigning the city and integrate smart solutions for the benefit of everyone!

First date of publication: December 23, 2016

Creative industries and the invisible hand

Policy making in the Netherlands[70]
From 2003 onwards, creative industries slowly gained the attention of politicians and policy makers in the Netherlands: creative industries as a sector was recognized as one of the key areas of the Dutch economy. First support and policy experiments started in 2005.

In the years after from 2007 the first national initiatives arose. Large national research programmes were started in the areas of games & ICT (GATE), cultural heritage & ICT (CATCH), and design (CRISP). Next to research, creative platforms, such as PICNIC and the Dutch Design Week, were initiated, organizing the sector and representing a broad creative network and as such communication channel for policy makers.

In 2011, the Dutch government supported nine topsectors, including Creative Industries. National strategic research agendas were developed, next to policy on human capital development and internationalization strategies. Cross-overs were actively stimulated by the topsector Creative Industries since 2015. In 2019, all topsectors in the Netherlands, including Creative Industries, started active collaboration on societal challenges: energy transition and sustainability, agriculture, water and food, health and care, and safety.

Market failure and policy instruments
One of the challenges in government support and policy making is that policy instruments have mainly been based on (applied) research. When support comes close to the market this would not be allowed anymore because of (illegal) state aid. So-called 'technology-readiness levels' (TRL) are widely used to determine whether aid can be legitimate. However, discussion about the usage of TRL in different (non-technology) contexts is ongoing.

Every two years, the Dutch organization for scientific research (NWO) develops calls and instruments, based on strategic research agendas from the topsectors. Furthermore, both the Ministry of Economic Affairs and the Ministry for Education,

Science and Culture have developed instruments for networking- and coordinating activities.

Next to generic instruments, some instruments are geared at a specific group, such as the instrument UPSTREAM.[72] UPSTREAM supports collaboration between performers, producers and designers, working on new applications in design of visual culture and technology in music. Another experimental instrument is IDOLS, supporting cross-overs and collaboration in consortia working on solutions for societal challenges.

> **IDOLS**[73]
>
> *"IDOLS (Increasing Demand by Offering LearningS) has been developed in the context of the labor market agenda for Cultural and Creative Industries. An instructing party or client experiences in what manner creative professionals contribute to societal challenges. At the same time the creative professional learns in what way collaboration in consortia proves to be successful for all parties.*
>
> *The good practices derived from these projects showcase successful collaboration, inspires, and supports the position of creative professionals and thus the competitive edge from the cultural and creative sector. The societals challenges are complementary to Dutch government policy priorities, such as safety, health and care, energy transition and sustainability, agriculture, water and food."*

European instruments
At a European scale, the European Commission supported cultural and creative industries for many years already. Creative Europes is a European framework program aiming at the cultural and audiovisual sectors. Creative Europes builds upon the previous Cultural Program and MEDIA Program.[74] The budget is 1.46 billion euro. Next to culture and media, this program knows a cross-sector strand.

Cultural heritage is another topic that has known many large programs for many years by the European Union, making use of a range of European policies, programs and funds. Between 2007-2013 4.5 billion euro was invested in cultural heritage via different programs[75], including funds from the European framework programs.

Towards a Knowledge and Innovation Community
End of 2018, the European Parliament reserved 3 billion euro for 'a cluster for an inclusive and creative society' in the new to be developed nineth European framework program.[76] One year later the ambition was translated into a new Knowledge and Innovation Community (KIC) for Cultural and Creative Industries, as part of the European Institute of Technology (EIT) 2020-2027 strategy.[77]

KIC CREATIVE AND CULTURAL INDUSTRIES[78]

"Plans to launch Europe's new creative and cultural industries' Knowledge and Innovation Community will be presented today, October15, 2019, in Budapest at INNOVEIT. This is part of the European Commission's plans for the EIT's 2021-2027 strategy that includes a 25 per cent budget increase to 3 billion euro.

By giving new opportunities to the 12.5 million Europeans employed in the EU's creative and cultural sector - that is 7.5 per cent of all employment in the EU economy - the EIT's new Knowledge and Innovation Community will be of strategic importance to powering innovation in the creative and cultural sectors.

Total turnover of the performing arts sector in Europe (including live music) is worth more than 32 billion euro. The performing arts sector is the largest employer among the creative and cultural sector in Europe, employing 1.25 million people. Over three quarters of employees are creators and/or performers.

The audio-visual and multimedia sector has seen tremendous growth in Europe. Activities related to the publishing of computer games saw compound average growth of more than 25 per cent in terms of total gross value added over the period 2008-2016. The creative and cultural sector's economic weight is comparable to that of ICT and the accommodation and food services sectors yielding more than 4 per cent of EU GDP."

The invisible hand is not sufficient

Adam Smiths' concept of the invisible hand[79] proved to work in ideal market circumstances. However, real life is more complicated than to leave everything to the market, next to fluctuations in the economy. Therefore, government regulation and support is desired to some extent. These market interventions vary along the diversity in cultural and creative sectors with regard to size, background, and characteristics, for different regions or countries.

Support, regulation (e.g. intellectual property rights), and instruments for cultural and creative industries need scale. The European Commission can really help this sector to make a large step and have impact, both from an economic and societal perspective. A knowledge and innovation community (KIC) will strongly contribute to the development of cultural and creative sectors in the years to come. This is even more important in times of corona, where the invisible hand won't bring us any further!

First date of publication: May 12, 2020

Mainstreaming benefits of the Cultural and Creative Sectors

A Plea for Potentials and Priorities of Cultural and Creative Sectors in the Research Framework Programme 9

The previous 8th European Research Framework Program Horizon 2020 (FP 8) focused on societal challenges and priorities. All the successful impacts of FP 8 do not make up one structural disadvantage: spill-overs did not gain interest adequate to its potential, while many innovations result from cross-overs between disciplines. The Cultural and Creative Sectors (CCS) have proven to be a vehicle to stimulate these cross-overs.

Especially at the interface of cultural and creative sectors and digital technologies, both break-through and incremental innovations can be effectively supported. The range of possible applications is manyfold, for instance in health and well-being, mobility, green energy and climate change. The NICE Award[80] showcases best practices of such spill-over innovations since 2014. The Digital R&D Fund for the Arts by NESTA and the Arts Council England[81] is a role model for funding instruments to mainstream innovation at cross-overs of CCS and digital technology. There is a need to support such spill-overs at a European level as well.

Funding cross-innovation in its social, not just technology, dimension is also paramount to an open society in Europe: cultural stakeholders in Europe have extensive practice and knowledge of social innovations, but they are too often limited to local boundaries. Mainstreaming local innovations transnationally and trans-culturally would support quick concrete problem-solving in Europe, especially for the unemployed youth. It would also support an open and diverse Europe politically. The National Alliance for Arts, Health and Well-being is such an example.[82]

A new priority
The European Creative Business Network (ECBN)[83] proposes to make the cultural and creative sectors a priority in FP 9. The FP 8 model has enabled first and great steps to promote CCS. In the future, however, it needs to take multiple dimensions to unleash the full value of CCS - of which cross-innovation is just one.

The economic size and societal importance of CCS with 12 million full-time jobs, which amounts to 7.5 % of the EU's work force, and approximately 509 billion euro in value added to GDP, can only fully support the future of Europe with a new strategic priority within Research Framework Programme 9 (FP 9).

The new Research FP 9 strategy must include at least a priority for cross-innovation of CCS. Whether this is by integrating CCS in the existing challenges or by creating a new challenge is up to policy makers and the EU administration. Given the relevance of start-ups and SMEs in CCS for urban development and industrial leadership, the benefits of CCS could also be mainstreamed in Europe through an own challenge. How to foster the disruptive innovation by CCS - hardly within an old economy challenge? How to find new technologies driven by cultural creative content - hardly with a technology challenge ?

Also calls are in most of the cases too abstract and too far away from the markets of the creative industries. Continuously open calls with cut-off dates should be given priority over singular calls in order to provide for continuity. Long-term programs would allow for a better planning from the perspective of creative companies.

Size matters
Given the innovation intensity in Cultural and Creative Sectors, it is adequate to invest at least 1 billion euro in Research and Development, that is 2% of its GDP of 509 billion euro. In comparison: The German CCS invest in innovation approximately 4,8 billion euro each year as the CCS Monitoring Report 2017 of the German Federal Ministry for Economy and Energy proofs.[84] This equals 4,85% of the CCS value added of 98,8 billion Euro in 2016. Is the European Union able to live up to the sectors requirements? Obviously the budget of FP 9 is large enough to invest 1 billion euro in CCS, but are insight and vision great enough?

Christian Ehler, MEP, Co-Chair of the Intergroup for Cultural Creative Sectors and Member of the Committee on Industry, Research and Energy, has been driving the agenda for creative industries[85] and comments the current discussions on FP 9 in May 2018:

"CCIs are at the heart of the European industry. They have to be able to profit from the benefits of research like any other industry. CCIs are breakthroughs, potentials and full of surprises for new ideas. They will be the most promising addition to the new research framework program (Horizon Europe) to be made."

Today spill-over effects and cross-innovation of CCS are the focus, but one must not forget the simple basis of the CCS: it is content production. As much as technology sectors need investments in new materials, CCS needs investment in content. Content - especially as big-data platforms thrive on content - is the conveyor belt of the 21st-century.

Concluding, CCS add substantial value to both Europe's economy and society in two directions: direct economic growth and large-scale spill-over effects. The new FP 9 is an opportunity for Europe to break the vicious circle of discussions about lacking evidence or inadequate evaluation and invest in CCS as a driver for innovation. Around 12 million employees in CCS across Europe are awaiting policy action!

First date of publication: June 4, 2018
Authors: Bernd Fesel (ECBN) and Frits Grotenhuis

Future perspectives

Since 2002, cultural and creative industries have taken a flight in terms of attention, support, and growth in numbers of employment and organizations. Cultural and creative industries worldwide flourished and improved our lives from a cultural, societal, and economical perspective.[86]

Cultural and creative industries have also had a strong influence on shaping our identity and the way we live. Creative methods such as design thinking, gamification, storytelling, and user-centered design provide alternative perspectives on innovation and societal challenges. In cross-over projects, cultural and creative industries proved to add value.[87]

Globalization and digitalization as major trends have had a large impact on today's lives. However, with Covid-19 as a major game changer, the current equilibrium and status quo will change.

After the first shock, with a strong rise in unemployment and growing nationalism, the world is looking for new growth paths.

Cultural and creative industries will add value in defining new directions, balancing society, economy, and sustainability. In addition, the role of the government will increase after decades of believe in the invisible hand of Adam Smith.[88] After decades of globalization, this process will probably be hampered, or maybe accelerated by cultural and creative innovations in governance? The role of creative governance and even bureaucracies will be central to the change capacity of societies in Europe - and thus the ability of Europe to keep her competitive advantage globally. New directions in society and economy need innovations in governmental systems first - and the cultural and creative industries are a change maker here too.

Digitalization, however, will gain relevance, also for the cultural and creative sector. Making use of big data can help designers (think of data-driven design in Philips healthcare products) or media specialists (think of data visualization or Google analytics) develop tailorized solutions. Artificial intelligence is driven by big data and will thus take a rise the coming years.

Furthermore, climate change makes decarbonization and the green economy a top priority, not only for sectors like housing or mobility, but across all sectors. A new economy model is about to become reality, the circular economy. In 2020 the European Green Deal and Covid19-Recovery Funds of the EU-Commission will focus on this circular transformation and make the circular economy the new mainstream of 21st century. A new dimension and boost of cross-innovations by the cultural and creative industries will be the result - which will also transform the cultural and creative industries itself.

Several scenarios have been pictured already, such as the European Creative Business Network balancing between the duration of the Covid-19 crisis (optimistic versus pessimistic) and global relations (local and closed versus global and open).[89] Strong lobbies have been initiated at local, regional, national, and European scale to support the basis of cultural and creative industries.

Cultural and creative industries are very vulnerable in crises like Covid-19, with their long tail of small and medium sized enterprises. Government aid is necessary and legitimate. At the same time, cultural and creative industries as a sector is very innovative and flexible. As such, this sector will be one of the enablers of the upcoming circular economy, the new mainstream after the corona crisis, and will help shaping a sustainable society with a new narrative.

Authors: Frits Grotenhuis and Bernd Fesel (ECBN)

Contributing authors

Dr. Frits Grotenhuis (1972) is strategy consultant and author, working in the triangle of higher education, government and industry. Frits' fields of expertise and interest are in digitalization and artificial intelligence, as well as cultural and creative industries.

Since creative industries gained political weight and policy attention in the Netherlands in 2004, Frits Grotenhuis has been involved in this relevant and strategic area of innovation. Frits was co-initiator of several regional, national and international initiatives and ecosystems, e.g. the national ICT-Innovation platform Creative Industries (IIP/Create), and the Topconsortium for Knowledge and Innovation of the topsector Creative Industries (TKI CLICKNL). In 2020, Frits was quartermaster for the platform Creative Economy for the Confederation of Netherlands Industry and Employers (VNO-NCW). Since 2020, Frits has been member of the Advisory Board of Fontys University of Applied Sciences – Academy for Creative Industries.

Over the years, Frits Grotenhuis has published several books, many blogs and articles on creative industries, amongst others in the International Journal of Cultural and Creative Industries. The last few years, Frits was moderator at the annual summits for the European Creative Business Network (ECBN) in Brussels, Vienna and Helsinki. This book reflects on some of these associations.

Bernd Fesel, director of the European Creative Business Network (ECBN), contributed to two chapters in this book. He is member of the Content Innovation Council of the Bookfair Frankfurt and served at the Board of European network on cultural management and policy (ENCATC) from 2015 to 2017. Bernd Fesel studied in Economics and Philosophy in Heidelberg and Bonn and graduated with an economist degree.

ECBN is a unique not for profit foundation, founded in 2011 with over 100 members in all EU countries. It promotes the interests of the cultural and creative industries in Europe.

Contact details

Frits Grotenhuis
frits@grotenhuisadviseert.nl
www.grotenhuisadviseert.nl

Bernd Fesel
bernd@ecbnetwork.eu
http://ecbnetwork.eu

List of abbreviations

ADHD	Attention Deficit/Hyperactivity Disorder
AOD	Academy of Design
ArtEZ	Hogeschool voor de Kunsten Arnhem, Enschede, Zwolle
CCIs	Cultural and Creative Industries
CCS	Cultural and Creative Sectors
DNA	Deoxyribonucleic acid
ECBN	European Creative Business Network
ECIS	European Creative Industries Summit
EIT	European Institute of Technology
eSOS	emergency Sanitation Operating System
EU	European Union
EY	Ernst and Young
FP	European Research Framework Program
GDP	Gross Domestic Product
GNP	Gross National Product
HAN	Hogeschool Arnhem Nijmegen
HKU	Hogeschool voor de Kunsten Utrecht
HU	Hogeschool Utrecht
IAA	International Motor Show
IBM	International Business Machines Corporation
ICT	Information and Communication Technology
IDOLS	Increasing Demand by Offering LearningS
IIP/Create	ICT-Innovation platform Creative Industries
IPR	Intellectual Property Rights
KIC	Knowledge and Innovation Community
MAS	Museum aan de Stroom
MEP	Member of European Parliament

MKB Nederland	Midden- en kleinbedrijf Nederland
MOOC	Massive Open Online Course
NRC	Nieuwe Rotterdamse Courant
NWO	Dutch organization for scientific research
3P's	People, Planet, and Profit
PhD	Doctor of Philosophy
R&D	Research & Development
ROC	Regionaal Opleidingencentrum
SLDF	Sri Lanka Design Week
SMEs	Small- and Mediumsized Enterprises
STHLM	Stockholm
SXSW	South By Southwest
TKI CLICKNL	Topconsortium for Knowledge and Innovation of the topsector creative industries
TRL	Technology-Readiness Levels
UAE	United Arab Emirates
UMCU	University Medical Center Utrecht
UNHCR	United Nations Refugee Agency
UK	United Kingdom
USA	United States of America
VNO-NCW	Confederation of Netherlands Industry and Employers
VR	Virtual Reality

References

1 http://ecbnetwork.eu

2 http://www.grotenhuisadviseert.nl

3 Rutten, P., O. Koops en F. Visser (2019). Monitor Creatieve Industrie 2019 Nederland, Top-10 steden, creatieve bedrijven en beroepen, stichting Media Perspectives, Hilversum, december

4 https://www.consilium.europa.eu/media/42770/ st06426-en20.pdf

5 SER en Raad voor Cultuur (2017). Passie Gewaardeerd: Versterking van de arbeidsmarkt in de culturele en creatieve sector, 21 april

6 https://www.bna.nl/nieuws/rijksbouwmeester-en-ontwerp-sector-willen-ruimtelijke-opgaven-samen-oppakken

7 Driessen, C. (2020). Noodplan voor artiest en componist, NRC, 30 maart

8 https://www.rijksoverheid.nl/actueel/nieuws/2020/03/17/ coronavirus-kabinet-neemt-pakket-nieuwe-maatregelen-voor-banen-en-economie

9 https://twitter.com/fedci/status/1244702978453487616?s=21

10 Rutten, P., O. Koops en F. Visser (2019). Monitor Creatieve Industrie 2019 Nederland, Top-10 steden, creatieve bedrijven en beroepen, stichting Media Perspectives, Hilversum, december

11 https://ucreate.nl

12 https://ucreate-weconnect.nl/poko-eindevent/

13 http://www.mind-labs.nl

14 https://futuremakers.artez.nl

15 https://www.madeinarnhem.nl/arnhem-is/creatief/

16 https://stateoffashion.org/en/visit/exhibition-searching-new-luxury/

17 Brochure 'State of Fashion 2018', introduction

18 https://www.researchgate.net/profile/Katja_Ruutu/publication/285596465_Cultural_Industries_in_Russia/links/5661979c08ae192bbf8a14a3/Cultural-Industries-in-Russia.pdf?origin=publication_detail

19 http://ac.gov.ru/en/events/014530.html

20 http://ac.gov.ru/en/events/014530.html

21 https://spb.hse.ru/international/sumsch/creativeindustries#pagetop

22 https://creativeconomy.britishcouncil.org/blog/12/07/01/moscow-clusters/

23 http://www.cisac.org

24 http://www.worldcreative.org/wp-content/uploads/2015/12/CulturalTimes_Regions.pdf

25 http://www.worldbank.org/en/news/feature/2017/01/25/mentoring-the-creative-industries-sector-in-kuwait

26 https://gulfnews.com/opinion/thinkers/dubai-innovates-for-a-vibrant-creative-economy-1.1624983

27 https://gulfnews.com/news/uae/shaikh-mohammad-launches-uae-cultural-development-fund-creative-industries-contributions-index-1.2168875

28 Florida, R. (2002). The rise of the creative class: And how it is transforming work, leisure, community and everyday life, New York: Basic Books

29 http://www.jordantimes.com/news/local/int'l-experts-high-light-potential-creative-industries

30 Glassman, James K. (November 23, 2009). "Where Tech Keeps Booming In Israel, a clustering of talent, research universities and venture capital." Wall Street Journal. Retrieved April 4, 2011

31 https://www.startupnationcentral.org

32 https://www.intheblack.com/articles/2017/11/01/israel-start-up-nation

33 https://www.startupnationcentral.org/opportunities/creative-business-cup-competition-2018/

34 Astana Contemporary Art Center, 'Artists & Robots', brochure, 2017

35 http://www.culturalentrepreneur.se/category/the-swedish-council-of-cultural-and-creative-industries/

36 https://stockholm.impacthub.net

37 https://sthlm-tech-fest-2018.confetti.events

38 "South By Southwest dedicates itself to helping creative people achieve their goals. Founded in 1987 in Austin, Texas, SXSW is best known for its conference and festivals that celebrate the convergence of the interactive, film, and music industries": https://www.sxsw.com

39 https://www.me-convention.com/en/mercedes-benz/events/me-convention/

40 https://pages.eiu.com/rs/753-RIQ-438/images/The_Global_Liveability_Index_2018.pdf

41 Seventh Austrian Creative Industries Report – Focus: Cross-over Effects and Innovation, Kreativwirtschaft Austria

42 http://www.viennadesignweek.at/?lang_id=en

43 http://ecbnetwork.eu/mainstreaming-benefits-of-the-cultural-and-creative-sectors/

44 Fernandopule, L. (2018), 'China's Asian model of development to benefit Sri Lanka', Sunday Observer, 11 November

45 http://sensemi.com

46 http://www.startextile.lk

47 http://www.hirdaramani.com

48 http://www.island.lk/index.php?page_cat=article-details&page=article-details&code_title=131268

49 https://www.aod.lk

50 https://www.srilankadesignfestival.com

51 https://www.mbfwsrilanka.com

52 https://www.effectivealtruism.org

53 http://www.publicdomainarchitecten.nl/en/drijvend-paviljoen/

54 http://waag.org/en/project/fairphone

55 https://www.unesco-ihe.org/news/smart-esos-toilet-emergencies

56 http://www.whatdesigncando.com/about-what-design-can-do/

57 Vinitsky, M., ed. (2017). 3.5 Square Meters: Constructive Responses to Natural Disasters, Hirmer Publishers

58 http://www.de-escalate.nl

59 Neumeijer, M. (2012) Metaskills: Five Talents for the Robotic Age, New Riders

60 Pijbes, W. (2019). "Wereldwijd is het museum in opmars, vooral in de Golfstaten", NRC, 20 maart

61 https://www.worldtravelawards.com/award-europes-leading-tourist-attraction-2019

62 https://nos.nl/artikel/2258917-miljoen-bezoekers-voor-louvre-abu-dhabi.html

63 https://www.nu.nl/cultuur-overig/5786070/rijksmuseum-wil-net-als-tropenmuseum-koloniale-roofkunst-teruggeven.html

64 https://www.britishmuseum.org/about_us/news_and_press/statements/parthenon_sculptures.aspx

65 Brochure British museum, Summer 2019

66 https://www.ed.nl/eindhoven/kwartiermaker-rijksmuseum-voor-design-eindhoven-museum-is-niet-een-gebouw~aa525ba5c/

67 Florida, R. (2002). The rise of the creative class: And how it is transforming work, leisure, community and everyday life, New York: Basic Books

68 Florida, R. (2017). The New Urban Crisis: How Our Cities Are Increasing Inequality, Deepening Segregation, and Failing the Middle Class-and What We Can Do About It, Oneworld Publications

69 Nijkamp, J.E. (2016) Counting on Creativity. The Creative Class as Antidote for Neighborhood Decline: the case of Rotterdam, PhD thesis, Erasmus University Rotterdam, 16 December

70 Grotenhuis (2015). Ups-and-downs in Creative Industries: Public-Private Partnerships from Key-area to Topsector, Soest, Netherlands: FDJ Grotenhuis (publisher), August

71 https://waag.org/en/project/picnic-festival

72 https://stimuleringsfonds.nl/nl/subsidies/deelregeling_upstream_music_x_design/

73 http://dutchcreativeindustries.nl/2019/06/17/fci-lanceert-idols/

74 https://ec.europa.eu/programmes/creative-europe/about_en

75 https://ec.europa.eu/culture/policy/culture-policies/cultural-heritage_en

76 http://ecbnetwork.eu/a-new-programme-for-an-inclusive-and-creative-society-with-30-billion-euro/

77 https://eit.europa.eu/who-we-are/eit-glance/eit-strategy-2021-2027

78 https://eit.europa.eu/news-events/news/eit-turns-volume-creative-cultural-industries

79 https://en.wikipedia.org/wiki/Invisible_hand

80 https://www.e-c-c-e.de/nice-award-2017.html

81 https://www.nesta.org.uk/project/digital-rd-fund-arts

82 http://www.artshealthandwellbeing.org.uk/resources/research

83 http://ecbnetwork.eu

84 http://www.kultur-kreativ-wirtschaft.de/KUK/Redaktion/DE/Publikationen/2017/monitoring-wirtschaftliche-eckdaten-kuk-2017.html

85 https://www.europarl.europa.eu/doceo/document/A-8-2016-0357_EN.html?redirect

86 https://ec.europa.eu/culture/policy/cultural-creative-industries_en

87 Grotenhuis, F.D.J. (2017). Value creation with Creative Industries Cross-overs in the Netherlands, International Journal of Cultural and Creative Industries, Vol. 4, Issue 3, pp. 52-61, July

88 https://en.wikipedia.org/wiki/Invisible_hand

89 http://ecbnetwork.eu/wp-content/uploads/2020/04/
    White_Paper_ECBN_CCI_Covdi9_20200408.pdf

90 http://ecbnetwork.eu